Aaron and Gayla's Alphabet Book

pictures by Jan Spivey Gilchrist
written by Eloise Greenfield.

Aaron and Gayla's
Alphabet Book

Aa

My name is Aaron.

Bb

I sit beside the window.

Cc

I drive my car.

Dd

I dig a hole.

Ee

I **eat my dinner.**

Ff

I look **for** **a** friend.

Gg

My name is Gayla.

Hh

I hide **my toys under the bed.**

Ii

I look **in** the big hole.

Jj

I jump over the puddle.

Kk

I **kick** the ball.

Ll

I look for a friend.

Mm

We meet.

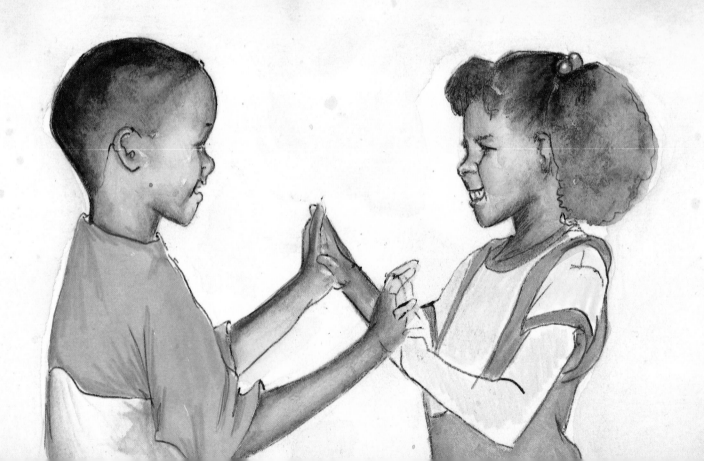

Nn

We make **noise.**

Oo

We open **an** old **box.**

Pp

We play together.

Qq

We quarrel.

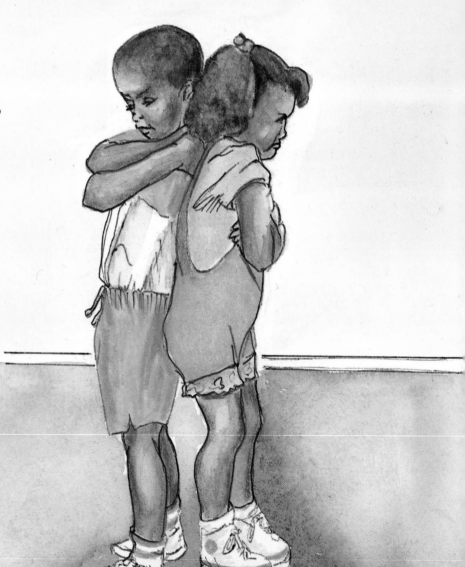

Rr

We run.

Ss

We **sit** beside each other.

Tt

We play **play** together.

Uu

We look under the bed.

Vv

We visit **the teddy bear.**

Ww

We **play together.**

Xx

We x-ray the teddy bear.

Yy

We yawn.

Zz

We snore. Zzzzzz.

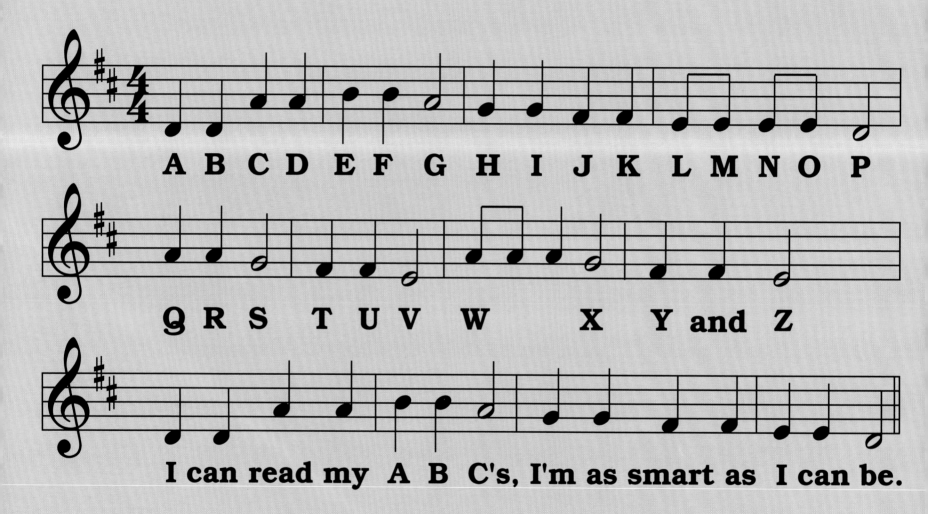